60
Words or Phrases
Commonly Misused by
ESL/EFL Students
Preparing for Universities

Kenneth Cranker

WAYZGOOSE PRESS

Sixty Words or Phrases Commonly Misused by ESL/EFL Students Preparing for Universities
Copyright © 2014 by Wayzgoose Press

ISBN 13: 978-1-938757-13-6
ISBN 10: 1938757130

Text by Kenneth Cranker.
Edited by Dorothy E. Zemach. Book and cover design by DJ Rogers.
Published in the United States by Wayzgoose Press.

To the Teacher

The material in this book was not designed to be a course in and of itself; it was designed to supplement courseware that reviews sentence-level grammar primarily for students who may be conditionally admitted to English-speaking universities, but whose grammar is insufficiently developed to matriculate. It was necessitated by the fact that at high levels of proficiency, because of the vocabulary required, grammatical issues tend to be as much related to word usage as they are to sentence structure. The collection of words/phrases in this book is derived from countless observations of erroneous word-level usage in student writings.

The number of phrases included in this work, sixty, is chosen for study at a rate of two per day over six weeks of classes. That rate allows it to adequately supplement but not dominate a course for general grammar review. It also prevents overload and enables students to digest and internalize the concepts and usage.

Each page includes a word/phrase with its part(s) of speech indicated, some italicized examples of erroneous usage, some italicized examples of correct usage, a brief summary ("in a nutshell") of the concepts involved, and a space for the creation of sentences using the featured expressions in specified ways. The erroneous usage is included for students to first identify whether they themselves make those sorts of errors, and then to analyze, discover what is wrong, and possibly discuss why it is incorrect (using language to describe the grammatical difficulty). This "languaging" can be extremely useful for internalizing grammatical concepts. Only after students have inductively reasoned through the erroneous usage should they examine the correct sentences and see how they exemplify proper usage. Then they should try to construct a summary themselves before checking the "in a nutshell" section. Finally, they should create their own sentences, pushing themselves to write in a sophisticated, academic (impersonal, at least) style.

There may be several ways for this procedure to work itself out in the classroom, but one way that works is to assign two pages for homework, and then in class briefly discuss the erroneous and correct sentences, elicit student summaries, and finally invite students to share their sentences on the whiteboard or in some other fashion. The class can then critique the sentences not only for correct usage of the target expressions but also for overall sentence level grammaticality, sophistication, and meaning. This process may take 15-20 minutes each day.

A suggested method of testing would be to provide two expressions that had been studied and to require students to create one impersonal, sophisticated sentence incorporating both expressions.

To the Student

Grammar is much more than verb tenses, articles, clauses, and word order. The challenge for university-bound or intermediate to advanced level writers is to use words and their various forms appropriately. For example, perhaps you have misused the noun *analysis* where you should have used the verb *analyze*. This is the type of word-level grammar that this book addresses.

This book contains 60 words/phrases that are commonly misused by writers striving for university level English proficiency. It is suggested that they be studied at the rate of about two per day for smooth acquisition, but you may find that you do not struggle at all with some of them. If that is the case, go on to the next one. By all means, do not pay too much attention to the errors other students tend to make and pick them up!

On each page, check out the examples of misuse, and if you can identify with the error, having made such errors in the past, then continue reading to understand why the errors are incorrect. Then read and re-read the correct examples to understand and deeply absorb how the expressions are properly used. Once you have done that, try to verbalize (put into words) the concepts you understood and compare your understanding with what is described in the "in a nutshell" section on each page. Finally, create your own sentences with an impersonal, academic tone using the expression in the ways that are specified, and find someone to check them for you for feedback.

These expressions are certainly not the only ones commonly misused by relatively highly proficient multilingual writers of English, but if you can use these 60 properly, your writing will be much more likely to be acceptable to university instructors and other readers.

Table of Contents

 **1**

According to (prep)

Misused
---

1. *According to Smith, he stated that insufficient sleep is a common problem.*
   (Only the fact is necessary. There is no need for a reporting verb.)

2. *The student was unable to pass according to his grades.*
   (It sounds as if the grades reported something.)

Correct
---

1. ***According to*** *Freud, dreams represent suppressed or repressed impulses.*

2. *The experiment was run **according to** the protocol established by Baker (2010).*

3. *Many religions believe rewards in the afterlife will be received **according to** good deeds done in this life.*
   (Less common usage)

In a nutshell: A stated fact usually follows *according to*. Basically, *according to* ___ means ___ *reported that…* . It can also mean *following* or, less commonly, *in accord with*.

Try writing your own sentences with *according to,* illustrating two different meanings.

According to Wechat, my friend is in the office.

This dish is made according to a secret recipe.

2 Acknowledge (v_t)

Misused

1. *Students must acknowledge much new information in college.*
   (*Acknowledge* does not mean to learn or to gain knowledge.)

2. *Michael Jordan was acknowledged to play basketball.*
   (The meaning is unclear. Was he acknowledged for his excellence in basketball, or did someone acknowledge that he had played basketball?)

3. *Albert Einstein is acknowledged greatest scientist ever.*
   (Two words are missing after *acknowledged*; you need *as the*.)

Correct

1. *The researcher **acknowledged** his technician who conducted most of the experiments in the paper that was published.*
   (= gave credit to)

2. *The politician **acknowledged that** he had committed an indiscretion.*
   (= confessed) 众所周知的

3. *Michael Jordan **is acknowledged by** many as the greatest basketball player ever.*
   (= recognized) 认可

In a nutshell: *Acknowledge* means "to give credit to" or "to confess/agree/recognize." In the passive voice, *as the* often follows *acknowledged*.

Try writing your own sentences, at least one for each meaning of *acknowledge* described above.

I acknowledge the truth of his statement.

The boy acknowledged that it is significant to be cautious with his words and deeds.

It feels comfortable to be acknowledged.

Against (prep)

Misused

---

1. *Many consumers against genetically modified foods (GMF).*
   (*Against* is not a verb.)

2. *The majority of voters are against to build new nuclear power plants.*
   (Because *against* is a preposition, the gerund *building* should be substituted or the infinitive *to build*.)

Correct

---

1. *Many consumers <u>oppose</u> genetically modified foods.*

2. *Many consumers are <u>opposed</u> to genetically modified foods.*

3. *Many consumers are **<u>against</u>** genetically modified foods.*
   (However, the *oppose* expressions are preferred as they are more academic.)

4. *The vast majority of voters are **<u>against</u>** constructing new nuclear power plants.*

5. *The board was leaning **<u>against</u>** the wall.*

In a nutshell: *Against* is not a verb. *Oppose* is. *Be against* means "oppose." *Against* is a preposition.

Try writing your own sentences, using *against* with two different meanings.

There should be a law against drugs.

He was sitting against the wall.

The law is against a great variety of drugs.

A great variety of drugs are against the law.

Agree (v$_i$)

Misused

1. *The executive agreed her advisor.*
   (needs *with*)

2. *The athlete agreed practicing more.*
   (needs an infinitive, not a gerund)

3. *The students agreed the new policy on academic honesty.*
   (needs a preposition)

Correct

1. *The executive **agreed with** her advisor.*

2. *The athlete **agreed to** practice more.*

3. *The students **agreed on/about** the new policy on academic honesty.*
   (This means they agreed with each other; it is unclear whether they support the policy.)

4. *The students **agree with** the policy.*
   (Here, they support the policy.)

5. *Some parents rarely argue and nearly always **agree**.*

In a nutshell: *Agree* can be followed by *with* and a person, or *to* and a verb, or *with/on/about* and an issue. If the subject is two parties, it can have nothing after it and mean *agree with each other*.

Try writing your own sentences using *agree with*, *agree to*, *agree on*, and *agree*.

We agree on this account.   The man agreed that this event was shocking.

A lot of people will agree with him.
↳ I agree with my teacher about/that; on
The boys agree to go ahead with the plan.

Almost (adv) / Most (adj/n)

Misused

1. *Almost students would prefer to study English abroad if they had the chance.* (What is an "almost student"? *Almost* needs a quantifier here. *Almost* is an adverb.)

2. *Most of the students progress only slowly when they study at home.* (What students are being referred to here? They are not specified.)

Correct

1. ***Almost** 70% of all international students would prefer to study English abroad if they had the chance.*

2. ***Most** students progress only slowly when they study at home.*

3. ***Most of the** students in this investigation progressed only slowly when they studied at home.*

4. *The coach **almost** committed a technical foul.* (*Almost* means nearly, but didn't.)

In a nutshell: *Almost* is an adverb, so it should be followed by a quantifier or a verb. *Most* means "the majority (of)" and can be followed by a plural noun or an *of* phrase with further specification.

Try writing your own sentences, one with *most*, one with *most of the*, and one with *almost*.

The boy has the most outlandish ideas.

Most of the uniforms got wet because of the rain.

The tree had almost been cut off.
                            down

Most

My of my students in the GLAD class taught by Ken.
      ↑
      determiners

Analyze (v$_t$) / Analysis (n)

Misused

1. *The analyze of the researcher was incorrect in three ways.*
   (*Analyze* is a verb, not a noun.)

2. *It is important to analysis the problem thoroughly before making a recommendation.*
   (*Analysis* is a noun, not a verb.)

3. *The analysises of the two economists differed greatly.*
   (The plural is *analyses*.)

Correct

1. *The **analysis** of the researcher was complete and insightful.*

2. *Before the committee could recommend a course of action, it had to **analyze** the situation thoroughly.*

3. *The **analyses** of the two economists differed greatly.*
   /iː/

In a nutshell: *Analyze* is a verb. *Analysis* is a noun. The plural is *analyses*.

Try writing your own sentences, one using the noun, one using the plural, and one using the verb.

The data was analyzed for two days.

This is a analysis from the crime scene

We tend to understand such analyses of our troubles.

✱ crux (the main point)

Aspect (n)

Misused

---

1. *The policy is flawed in several aspects.* ~~respects~~
   (*Respects* is a better word here, meaning "ways." *Aspects* means "faces," or possibly "parts.")

   aspect
   respect
   perspective

2. *The analysts examined the work from several aspects.* ~~respects~~
   (*Perspectives* is a more appropriate word.)

Correct

---

1. *Several **aspects** of the policy were flawed.*

2. *The analyst examined a number of **aspects** of the program.*

3. *Many **aspects** of the paper require revision.*

In a nutshell: *Aspect* means "a facet/face/part." It does not mean "way" or "point of view."

Try writing your own sentences with *aspect*.

Lighting is a vitally significant aspect of film-making.

8

handwritten annotations:
emotional waiting
At Last (waiting for a long time, take a lot patient)
Last (list)

F start of sequence, series

At first (adv) / First (adv/adj)

L change

Misused

1. *At first, sound waves are collected by the outer ear.*

2. *Firstly, water is cheaper than soda.*
   (*First* is already an adverb. This mistake is so common among native speakers that it is almost recognized as acceptable, especially in speech. In written language, however, many will find fault with it. Also, it is more sophisticated to incorporate *first* into a clause.)

Correct

1. ***First**, light enters the eye through the pupil.*

2. *The **first** reason for drinking more water is that it is less expensive than soda.*

3. ***At first** water may seem tasteless and boring, but in the end, it may be acknowledged as the best fluid to drink.*
   (*At first* implies a change.)

In a nutshell: *At first* indicates a state before a change. *First* indicates the start of a series. More sophisticated writing will integrate *first* into a clause.

Try writing your own sentences, one with *first* incorporated into a clause and one with *at first*.

Neil Alden Armstrong was the first man who walked on the moon.

At first the boy refused to accept any responsibility; however, he was trying (tried) to apologize at the last moment.

9 Aware (adj)

Misused

---

1. *Many students did not aware the Nobel Prize winner was on campus.*
   (*Aware* is an adjective, not a verb)

2. *The citizens awared the plane crash in the capital.*
   (*Aware* is not a verb.)

3. *The government was aware of that its citizens were hungry.*
   (*Aware of* would be followed by a noun or noun phrase, and *aware that* would be followed by a sentence, but either *of* or *that*, not both, should be used.)

Correct

---

1. *Few **were aware** (that) the Nobel Prize winner was on campus.*
   (*That* is optional here, but it is in the deep grammar.)

2. *The citizens **were aware of** the plane crash in the capital.*

3. *Most of the country **was aware that** a plane had crashed in the capital.*

In a nutshell: *Aware* is an adjective. It requires a *be* verb before it and an *of* prepositional phrase or a *that* clause after it.

Try writing your own sentences, one with *aware (that)* and one with *aware of.*

The girl was probably aware that she needed to make a conscientious effort to improve her grade.

Citizens are becoming increasingly aware of national issues in recent years.

10

Back (prep/v/n)

Misused

---

1. *After a few months of studying abroad, most international students hope to back to their home country.*
   (*Back* can be a verb, but it means "to go backward or in reverse," as with a car. It can also mean "to support." Here the verb *go* is needed. Better yet, *return* can be used instead of *go back*. It is more academic.)

Correct

---

1. *Most nations represented in the U.N.* **back** *the plan to reduce CO_2 emissions.*
   (*Back* means "support.")

2. *It is often difficult to* **back** *a truck into a parking space.*

3. *Most international students* **go back to** *their country after earning their degrees.*
   (Again, *return* would be better here.)

4. *There are relatively few sensory neurons in the skin of the human* **back**.

In a nutshell: While *back* can be a verb or a noun, it is most often a preposition that is part of phrasal verbs such as *go back* or *take back*. As a verb, it means "to support" or "to go backwards" like a car in reverse.

Try writing your own sentences, using *back* in at least three different ways.

Students should think back and realize how much better our life is now than before.

The answer again goes back to the ancient time.

Unfortunately, performing undo now merely brings back the one word.

Based on (prep phrase)

Misused

1. *Based on Smith (2009), global population has exceeded 7 billion.*
   (*According to* would be much better. The above sentence seems to be a statement of fact rather than a conclusion.)

2. *The fireworks were canceled based on the weather.*
   (*Because of* or *due to* would be more natural.)

Correct

1. ***Based on*** *figures and projections reported by Smith (2009), it is reasonable to conclude that global population has already exceeded 7 billion.*

2. ***Based on*** *the protocol established in 2001 for safely conducting fireworks, the council decided to cancel the firework display.*
   (*Based on* is best used with conclusions.)

3. *The movie **was based on** a bestselling novel.*

In a nutshell: *Based on* should be followed by evidence and a conclusion. It means "having as its basis."

Try writing your own sentences with *based on.*

The price should be based on the actual situation of the customers.

_____

_____

_____

_____

_____

_____

12 Cause (v$_t$/n)

Misused

---

1. *The error caused that many residents evacuated the area needlessly.*
   (*Cause* cannot take a *that* clause.)

2. *The food shortage caused many get sick.*
   (*Cause* is completed with an object – *many* here – and an infinitive. A *to* is necessary before *get*.)

3. *A virus caused sick.*
   (*Cause* can be completed with a simple direct object, but that must be a noun – *sickness*.)

Correct

Make	Let
cause	allow
force	permit
persuade	
command	
help	
enable	
encourage	

(to)

1. *The error **caused** many citizens to evacuate needlessly.*

2. *The food shortage **caused** many to get sick.*

3. *A virus **caused** the illness.*

4. *There were three primary **causes** for the epidemic.*

5. *The entrance exam **causes** millions of students stress.*
   (This is a shortened form of "causes stress for millions of students.")

In a nutshell: *Cause* ____ *to* + verb is a common construction. Don't forget the *to*. *Cause* can also be followed by a noun, usually a sort of problem. It cannot be followed by a *that* clause.

Try writing your own sentences, one using *cause* as a verb followed by an object and infinitive, one with *cause* as a verb with a simple object, and one with *cause* as a noun.

The earthquake caused great damage.

The cause of autism is unknown.

This disease can cause blindness.

Character (n) / characteristic (n/adj)

Misused

1. *Reliability and fuel efficiency are two important characters for cars.*
   (*Characteristics* is better. It means "traits.")

2. *The protagonist and the antagonist are the two main characteristics in the play.*
   (Here, the desired meaning is "people," so *character* is needed.)

3. *Education should not only provide knowledge, it should also produce characters.*
   (Here, *character*, meaning "balanced, mature, moral personality" is needed. It is not countable.)

Correct

1. *The **characteristics** valued most in abstracts are clarity and brevity.*

2. *The cartoon **characters** recognized most worldwide may be Tom, the cat, and Jerry, the mouse.*

3. *The company desires employees of sound **character**.*

4. *The secretary replied with his **characteristic** humor.*
   (Here, *characteristic* is an adjective meaning "typical of a person.")

In a nutshell: *Character* is always a noun, but it can mean "moral integrity" (non-count) or "role in a play" (count). *Characteristic* can be a countable noun or even an adjective.

Try writing your own sentences, one using *character* (non-count), one using *characters*, one using *characteristic* as a countable noun, and one using *characteristic* as an adjective.

Chinese characters adapted into the Japanese language.

My strongest characteristics ̶i̶s̶ are my cheerfulness and friendliness.

What characteristics should an actor own ?

They share the character flaw of arrogance.

Choose (v$_t$) / Chose (past) / Chosen (p.p.) / Choice (n/adj)

Misused

1. *The principal choosed a new desk for her office.*
   (*Chose* is the past tense.)

2. *It is difficult for undergraduates to chose among competing graduate programs.*
   (*Choose* is the base form of the verb used with infinitives).

3. *A newly elected president must choice his cabinet.*
   (*Choice* is a noun, not a verb.)

4. *The majors of many students are choosen by their parents.*
   (*Chosen* is the proper past participle.)

Correct

1. *The carpenter **chose** tools appropriate for the job.*

2. *There are so many models of cars that it is often difficult to **choose** one.*

3. *The **choice** between economic development and environmental protection is a difficult one.*

4. *London **was chosen** to be the city to host the summer Olympics after Beijing.*

5. *Only **choice** grapes are used to make this wine.*
   (*Choice* as an adjective means "of the finest quality.")

In a nutshell: The spelling is key. Two *o*'s is present tense; one *o* is past. *Choice* is a noun, or even an adjective.

Try writing your own sentences, using different forms of the verb *choose* and its related noun.

This company has many patterns in stock for costumers to choose from.

The students chose a committee to represent them.

This city chosen as host for the Olympic games.

He is the automatic choice for the senior team.

Compared (v$_t$) / Comparing

Misused

---

1. *Comparing with New York City, Tokyo is much cleaner.*
   (Should be *compared to.*)

2. *Compared the Nile and the Mississippi, the Nile is longer.*
   (Should be *comparing*, but, even *comparing* creates an awkward sentence because the subject of the main clause is not the one doing the comparing.)

3. *Compared to China, the population of the U.S. is smaller.*
   (This is not quite parallel. *Population* appears to be being compared to *China*.)

Correct

---

1. *Tokyo is extremely clean,* **compared to** *New York City.*
   (The deep grammar here is "if or when it is compared to"; thus, the passive form of *compare*, the past participle *compared*, is correctly used.)

2. **Comparing** *modern agricultural practices with those of 500 years ago reveals numerous stark differences.*

3. *When* **comparing** *the lengths of the world's greatest rivers, one finds that the Nile is longer than the Mississippi.*
   (This can be more simply stated as *The Nile is longer than the Mississippi.*)

4. **Compared to** *the population of China, that of the U.S. is smaller.*
   (*That of* means "the population of." The two populations are being compared.)

In a nutshell: Use *compared to. Comparing ... with* usually leads to awkward sentences at best. When comparing or contrasting, *that of* or *those of* is useful to maintain parallelism.

Try writing your own sentences using *compared*, *comparing*, and *that of* or *those of.*

My teacher compared the world to a stage.

Travelling on foot takes such a long time comparing with modern ways of getting about.

Compared to Ali, Howard is taller

Consider (v_t)

Misused

1. *The professor considered that the students who did not complete their assignments were lazy.*
   (Use *believed* or *thought*.)

2. *The defendant considered his attorney as a friend.*
   (*As* is unnecessary.)

Correct

1. *The judge did not* **consider** *the testimony relevant.*
   (*consider* + noun + adj)

2. *The professor* **considered** *students who graduated his colleagues.*
   (*consider* + noun + noun)

3. *The appeals court is* **considering** *whether to overturn the previous decision.*
   (consider + *wh-* clause)

In a nutshell: *Consider* basically means "think about" or "think that ___ is," so *that* clauses don't work well with it. *Consider* can take a noun and then another noun or an adjective after it.

Try writing your own sentences using *consider* + noun + adj and *consider* + noun + noun patterns.

We consider that the driver is not to blame.
He was considered to be a paragon of virtue.
These young people did quite well considering the circumstances.

_____

_____

_____

_____

17 Consist of (v$_i$)

Misused

1. *The peanut butter was consisted of only peanuts and salt.*
   (*Consist* cannot be made passive.)

2. *The soil consists in mostly clay.*
   (Use *of*, not *in*.)

3. *The student body consists mostly native English speakers.*
   (You always need *of* with *consist*.)

Correct

1. *Sea salt **consists of** sodium chloride and many other minerals.*

2. *The tour group **consisted of** tourists from seven different nations.*

In a nutshell: *Of* is used with *consist*, and *consist of* cannot be made passive or have a *be* verb in front of it.

Try writing your own sentences with *consist of*.

This electronic computer consists of five units although they are of different kinds.

Contact (v/n)

Misused

---

1. *The hospital contacted with the patient's parents as soon as they could.*
   (*Contact* is a transitive verb, so it will not take a preposition.)

2. *It is important to remain in contact to friends from college.*
   (*Contact* as a noun is part of the idiom *in contact with.*)

Correct

---

1. *The admissions office **contacted** the student immediately to let her know they had admitted her.*

2. *Electricity will flow through metal if it **contacts** an electric source.*

3. *The former president has stayed **in** constant **contact with** the present president.*

In a nutshell: As a verb, *contact* will not be followed by any preposition. As a noun, it will be followed by *with*.

Try writing your own sentences, one using *contact* as a verb and one using *contact* as a noun.

Friendly contacts between different people facilitate the cultural and economic interchange.

The girl contacted me as soon as she arrived.

Contacting with realities indisposed him to any more idle speculations

19

Dead (adj) / Died (past)

Misused

---

1. *The animal in the cage in the zoo was died.*
   (*Die* is an intransitive verb. It cannot be made passive, nor can it be used as an adjective. *Dead* should be used here.)

2. *The nation mourned when its greatest leader dead.*
   (Here, *died*, the past tense of *die*, is necessary.)

3. *A died skunk was lying in the road, so the entire neighborhood stank.*
   (The adjective *dead* should be used here.)

4. *The old man died for three weeks.*
   (*Die* refers to a point in time, the transition from being alive to being dead.)

Correct

---

1. *The whale that had washed up on the beach **was dead**.*

2. *The bear that fell out of the tree **died** from the fall.*

3. *Crows were eating the **dead** carcass on the side of the road.*

4. *The old man was thought to be **dying** for three weeks, but then he miraculously recovered.*

In a nutshell: *Died* is the past tense of a point-in-time verb. *Dead* is an adjective that describes something that has died. It is no longer alive.

Try writing your own sentences, one using the adjective *dead* and one using the verb *die*.

People knew nothing of the dead girl.

The girl died in misery in a convent.

Decide (v$_t$)

Misused

1. *Nutrition decides how long an individual might live.*
   (Sounds like "nutrition" is thinking and making a decision. *Determines* is a better choice.)

Correct

1. *It is difficult to **decide** which road to take, but the road taken may determine the future.*

In a nutshell: To *decide* something, in a strict sense, requires a brain. Animals or humans *decide* various affairs. Mindless events or facts *determine* outcomes. *Determine* can be used to mean *decide*, but not vice versa.

Try writing your own sentences, one using *decide* and one using *determine*.

They are trying to decide where to situate the hospital.

Helen was a determined girl who lost her legs when she was born.

21

Decline (v_t/v_i)

Misused

1. *The population of the town was declined over the last decade.*
   (*Decline*, meaning "fall, decrease," is intransitive and cannot be made passive.)

2. *The police officer was declined the bribe offered him, and arrested the traffic violator instead.*
   (*Decline*, meaning "refuse," is transitive. It can be made passive, but the passive is not constructed properly here.)

Correct

1. *World population **declined** dramatically during the years of WWII.*

2. *The guest **declined** the coffee that was offered to her.*

3. ***The decline** in economic growth has business and political leaders concerned.*
   (Here *decline* is used as a noun.)

4. *The bribe **was declined by** the police officer, and the traffic violator was arrested.*
   (Here the passive is formed correctly.)

In a nutshell: *Decline* can mean "to refuse" (transitive) or "to go down" (intransitive). Introducing a *be* verb before *decline* can change its meaning from "to go down" to " to refuse." In the passive voice, it must mean "to refuse."

Try writing your own sentences with *decline*, one meaning "refuse," one meaning "decrease," and one in the passive voice.

This dynasty walked up to decline and extinction.

The company declined to comment on this article.

22

Discuss (v$_t$)

Misused

1. *The classmates were discussing about the test they had just taken.*
   (*Discuss* is transitive and takes a direct object, so no preposition is necessary.)

2. *The villagers were discussing amongst themselves quietly.*
   (Again, *discuss* requires a direct object. Is there one in the above sentence?)

Correct

1. *The classmates were **discussing** how they had done on the previous test.*
   (*How they had done* is a noun clause that functions as the object of *discuss*.)

2. *The villagers started **discussing** the theft quietly amongst themselves, but soon their **discussion** became very animated.*

In a nutshell: *Discuss* and *about* do not go together.

Try writing your own sentences with *discuss*, one with a noun clause as its object and one with a simple noun or noun phrase as its object.

The ~~Suth~~ South Korean and American armed forces are thought to be discussing new rules of engagement ~~to allow this~~

Our discussion in ~~this~~ ~~per~~ the previous chapter continues this line of thinking.

23 Due to (prep)

Misused

1. *The mail arrived late due to the mail truck had a flat tire.*
   (*Due to* is completed with a noun, not a sentence, because *to* is a preposition. *Because* would be much better here.)

2. *The town was evacuated due to that the hurricane was approaching.*
   (If *that* followed *hurricane*, this sentence would be correct.)

Correct

1. *The mail arrived late **due to** a flat tire on the mail truck.*

2. *The town was evacuated **due to the fact that** a hurricane was approaching.*

3. *The evacuation was **due to** an approaching hurricane.*
   (Notice how sentence #3 is much more succinct than sentence #2, and therefore better.)

In a nutshell: *Due to* means "because of," not "because." It will be followed by a noun (phrase).

Try writing your own sentences, one with a simple noun phrase after *due to* and one that includes *the fact that*.

This accident was due to ~~r~~ Jame's negligence

~~Tom~~ Tom's recuperation ~~cancer~~ is due to the fact that he has a friend who has superpower.

24 Environment (n)

Misused

1. *Industrialization has caused numerous environment problems.*
   (*Environment* is a noun. Its adjective form is *environmental*, which would be more appropriate here.)

2. *It is necessary to pay more attention to environment; if it is destroyed, humans may not survive.*
   (There is only one universal macro-environment, so *the* is needed. Micro-environments do exist, but that is not the intended meaning here.)

Correct

1. ***Environmental*** *issues will be important in the upcoming election.*

2. *Excessive production of CO_2 may damage* ***the environment.***

3. *There is debate as to which factor is more significant to intellectual development,* ***environment*** *or genetics.*
   (Notice how this sentence uses *environment* in the "micro" sense. It differs with each person, and influences the way each person thinks.)

In a nutshell: The most common meaning of *environment* is the global environment, and there is only one, so *the* precedes it. The adjective form of *environment* is *environmental*.

Try writing your own sentences with the noun and adjective form of *environment*.

The research proves the persistance of huge environmental problems.

25

Even / Even if (conj) / Even though (conj)

emphasis

Misused

---

1. *Even this course is difficult, it is interesting and essential.*
   (Needs *though* after *even.*)

2. *Even though it rains tomorrow, the fundraising walk will be held.*
   (Tomorrow's weather is uncertain, so *if* should be used instead of *though.*)

3. *Even if the victim received emergency care, he died.*
   (Here, it seems that it was known that the victim did receive care, so *though* is better than *if.*)

4. *The doctors even did not know how to treat him.*
   (*Even* is in the wrong place. It should follow *not.*)

Correct

---

1. ***Even though*** *the course was difficult, it was enjoyable.* happened
   即使；虽然。

2. ***Even if*** *there is inclement weather, the fundraising walk will be held.* Not happen
   即使；虽然。

3. *The victim probably would have died **even if** he had received emergency care.*
   (This sentence implies that the victim did NOT receive emergency care.)

4. *The victim survived **even though** his wounds were serious.*

5. ***Even*** *the doctors were amazed at the victim's rapid recovery.*

In a nutshell: *Even if* is used with unknown circumstances, and *even though* is used with known ones. *Even* generally precedes the word it modifies.

Try writing your own sentences, one with *even* alone, one with *even if*, and one with *even though*.

Amy will be indignent even if we give her notebook back.

Even Ken can do that problem.

Ken even can do that problem.

26

Health (n) / Healthy (adj)

Misused

1. *Obesity is a major healthy problem in the U.S.*
   (This sentence seems to indicate that the problem is *healthy*. *Healthy* is an adjective that means "in good condition, not sick.")

2. *Healthy is a fundamental factor that determines happiness.*
   (The subject of the sentence should be the noun *health*.)

3. *Parents always hope their children will be health.*
   (Needs the adjective *healthy*.)

Correct

1. *Heart disease is the number one **health** issue in the U.S.*

2. ***Health** is determined by both genetic and environmental factors.*

3. *A well-known proverb states that a **healthy** child is a happy child, but there are many who disagree.*

4. ***Health foods** often contain surprising amounts of sugar or unusual oils.*
   (*Health foods* are foods that are designed to promote *health*. Experts often disagree as to whether or not they are truly *healthier* – better for *health* – than ordinary unprocessed foods.)

In a nutshell: *Health* is a noun, and *healthy* is an adjective.

Try writing your own sentences, one with the noun and one with the adjective form of *health*.

Kevin's health took a turn for the worse.

Animals need a healthy surrounding to survive.

Image (n) / Imagine (v) / Imagination (n)

Misused

1. *It is difficult to image a world without hunger.*
   (*Image* is a noun, not a verb. *Imagine* is necessary here.)

2. The imagine of the scene of the crime was etched in the mind of the witness.
   (Here the noun *image* is needed.)

3. *Children have a more creative images than adults.*
   (*Imagination*, the power to envision and create, is needed here.)

Correct

1. *It is not easy to **imagine** life without gravity.*

2. *The **image** of his mother's crying face haunted the criminal.*

3. *Walt Disney is famous for his **imagination**.*

4. *The goal of advertising is to promote the **image** of a company.*

In a nutshell: *Image* is a noun, meaning "picture," not a verb. *Imagine* is a verb. *Imagination* is the power of the brain to create new ideas and images.

Try writing your own sentences, one with *image*, one with *imagine*, and one with *imagination*.

Miao admired her image in the mirror.

The girl imagined her youth and beauty fading

Miao's imagination is too powerful that because she imagined her image will be a fad in the future in the mirror.

Impact (n/v$_t$)

Misused

1. *Hard work and discipline impact on results.*
   (*Impact* is a transitive verb, so it needs no preposition.)

2. *Teachers and parents have the greatest impact in the development of children.*
   (*Impact* as a noun takes the preposition *on*, not *in*.)

Correct

1. *Conscientiousness **impacts** longevity greatly.*

2. *The **impact** of conscientiousness **on** longevity should not be underestimated.*

3. *The entire moon shook from the **impact** of the meteor that struck it.*
   (Notice that there is no *on* in this sentence. It is understandable, though, that the meteor exerted a powerful *impact on* the moon.)

4. *Reducing CO_2 emissions might exert a significant **impact on** global temperatures, but there is no guarantee that it will.*

In a nutshell: *Impact* as a verb has no preposition after it. *Impact* as a noun may have an *of* phrase (describing what made the *impact*) and/or an *on* phrase (describing what *was impacted*).

Try writing your own sentences, one with the noun and one with the verb.

The movie impacts us in a multitude of ways

The impact of the comet killed all the dinosaurs.

29 Influence (n/v$_t$)

Misused

1. *Hard work and discipline influence on results.*
   (*Influence* here is a transitive verb, so it needs no preposition.)

2. *Teachers and parents have the greatest influence in the development of children.*
   (*Influence* here is a noun, and takes the preposition *on*, not *in*.)

Correct

1. *Did using the same sentences to illustrate the mistakes using "impact" and "influence"* **influence** *readers to understand that the two words are synonyms used in identical ways?*

2. *Perhaps having completed half of this book has already exerted a positive* **influence on** *their writing.*

3. *It is hoped that the* **influence** *of this book will not be merely a short-term one.*

In a nutshell: *Influence* follows the same pattern and has basically the same meaning as *impact*. The verb form has no preposition after it, and the noun form may have an *of* phrase (describing what made the impact) and/or an *on* phrase (describing what was impacted).

Try writing your own sentences, one with the noun and one with the verb.

Young people are quickly influenced by new ideas.

This event had a pernicious influence on society.

Instead of (prep)

Misused

---

1. *If vegetables are insteaded for junk food, blood sugar levels can be reduced.*
   (*Instead* is not a verb. Instead of "are insteaded for," use *replace* or
   are substituted for.)

Correct

---

1. *Diets are healthier if vegetables are eaten **instead of** junk foods.*

2. ***Instead of** processed foods, which often have less fiber and more salt,
   fruits and vegetables are recommended.*

In a nutshell: *Instead* is not a verb. *Instead of* forms a prepositional unit.

Try writing your own sentences with *instead* and *instead of.*

The ~~one~~ economy ⌄(of the company) is shrinking instead of growing.

Instead of kerosene lanterns, we have electricity.

I will travel to NY instead of DC.

Instead of travel to DC, I will go to NY.

I will not go to DC; I will go to NY instead.

Stress the last one.

D C

E L I

U C L A

N A A C P

☆ Ⓑ

I will <u>substitute</u> B <u>for</u> A.
replace A with B

31 It is hard / difficult / easy

Misused

1. *It is hard that an international student has to get an American driver's license.*
   (A *that* clause cannot complete this type of expression.)

2. *It is difficult that taking three exams in the same day.*
   (Without *that*, this sentence will work, but *Taking three exams in the same day is difficult* is a better written sentence.)

3. *Students are easy to contact professors by email.*
   (The students are not easy; contacting professors is.)

4. It is easy for people to forget.
   (*People* is not necessary – a simple infinitive can be used.)

Correct

1. ***It is hard for*** *an international student to obtain an American driver's license.*
   (Notice the *for* ___ *to* construction.)

2. ***It is easy for*** *Chinese students* ***to*** *eat with chopsticks.*

3. ***It is difficult*** *to take three exams in the same day.*
   (Notice the infinitive instead of a *that* clause, a gerund, or a people clause.)

4. ***It is easy for*** *students* ***to*** *contact professors by email.*

In a nutshell: *It is difficult/easy/hard* can be followed by a *for* ___ *to* construction, or a simple infinitive.

Try writing your own sentences, one with *easy* and one with *difficult*. Also try to create one sentence with *for* ___ *to* and one with an infinitive.

It is ~~hard~~ difficult for an inveterate smoker to give up tobacco.

It is difficult to remove overnight all the grievances accumulated over the years.

32

Lead ($v_t/v_i/n$)

Misused

1. *The criminal's anger toward society lead him to a life of crime.*
   (The past tense of *lead* is *led*.)

2. *The fall in oil prices led to the company go bankrupt.*
   (In this sentence, *company* has become acceptable, but in the deeper grammar, the word would be *company's*. That requires an object of the preposition *to*, which requires *go* to be the gerund *going*.)

3. *The publication* Common Sense *led many Americans support the revolution.*
   (*Lead* can take two objects, one a doer, and the other an infinitival action. The word *to* is needed before *support*.)

Correct

1. *The teacher **led** her students onto the bus.* (v_t)

2. *A terrible bout with the flu **led** to the student's requesting an incomplete.* (v_i)

3. *Video games may **lead** teenagers to become irresponsible and irritable.* (v_t)

4. *Each day a different student **leads** the discussion.* (v_t)

5. *The **lead** in sales enjoyed by that company is shrinking.* (n)

In a nutshell: *Lead* ___ *to* + verb is a common transitive construction. The *to* is necessary. *Lead to* (intransitive) will be followed by a noun because *to* is a preposition.

Try writing your own sentences, using *lead* as a v_i, as a v_t, and as a noun.

The polluted water lead fishes to die.

33 Lack (v$_t$/n)

Misused

1. *The vegetables did not grow because they lack of water.*
   (The past tense verb *lacked* is needed here instead of *of* + noun.)

2. *Water lacks on the moon.*
   (*Is lacking* would work, but not *lack*.)

3. *Many children misbehave because of lack attention.*
   (*They lack* would work in place of *of lack*, or *the lack of* would work in place of *lack*.
   Of is a preposition, so it requires a noun as an object, not a verb with an object
   of its own, as in *lack attention*. If *of* is eliminated, *because* can be completed
   with a clause.)

Correct

1. ***A lack of*** water retarded the growth of the vegetables.

2. *The moon **lacks** water.*

3. ***Lack of*** attention is a common cause of misbehavior among children.

4. *Funding **was lacking**, so the project came to a halt.*

In a nutshell: *Lack* requires an object, except with the intransitive expression *is lacking*. *Lack*
can also be a noun, in which case it will be followed by *of*.

Try writing your own sentences, one using *lack* as a verb and one using it as a noun.

These vegetables died ~~for~~ from lack of water.

Nothing is lacking for Miao's happiness.

A story that lacks spice makes the boy feel a sleepy.

Residents of metropolitan areas tend to lack exercise.

34

Lose (v$_t$) / Lost (past) / Loose (adj) / Loosen (v$_t$)

(handwritten above Loose: tight)

Misused

1. *Many adults need to lose their weight.*
   (*Lose weight* is idiomatic; no possessive pronoun is necessary.)

2. *The home team losed the game.*
   (The past tense of *lose* is *lost*, not *losed*.)

3. *Several tigers got lose in the circus and escaped.*
   (The adjective *loose* is needed here, not the verb *lose*.)

4. *The government should loose requirements on housing loans.*
   (The verb *loosen* is needed, not the adjective *loose*.)

5. *The taxi driver was lost his way, so he arrived late.*
   (*Lose* is a transitive verb, so the passive construction is incorrect here.)

Correct

1. *The patient **lost** considerable weight in the hospital.*

2. *The crowd was disappointed when the home team **lost** (the game).*

3. *The tiger that had gotten **loose** was tranquilized and captured.*

4. ***Loosening** requirements on housing loans might improve the housing market.*

5. *The taxi driver **got lost**, so she gave the rider a reduced fare.*
   (*Got lost = lost her way.*)

In a nutshell: *Lose* is a transitive verb, and its past tense is *lost*. *Loose* is an adjective meaning "not tight," and *loosen* means "to make loose."

Try writing your own sentences, one with *lose*, one with *lost*, one with *loose*, and one with *loosen*.

It is easy for a child to lose self-respect.

Domestic conditions did not justify loosening of monetary policy.

Need (v$_t$/n) / Require (v$_t$)

Misused
---

1. *An engineering degree needs many math and science courses.*
   (The degree does not need anything. Students may need to complete courses, though.)

2. *The university needs applicants to submit applications by April 1.*
   (This is a policy of the university, so it is a requirement of applicants, not a need of the university.)

Correct
---

1. *Attaining a degree in engineering* **requires** *intensive study, often for more than four years.*

2. *All mammals* **need** (or **require**) *oxygen to live.*

3. *Sunlight* **is needed** (or **is required**) *for photosynthesis.*

4. *The university* **requires** *every freshman to live in a dormitory.* (A rule)

In a nutshell: The subject of *need* is something that will not thrive without the needed item. While *require* may be used in that way, it has an additional usage in which a rule demands (*requires*) some sort of action. *Need* does not share this usage.

Try writing your own sentences, one with *need* and one with *require*.

The company needs to ~~service~~ serve the primordial ~~needs~~ requirements of the masses.

_____

_____

_____

_____

_____

_____

36

No matter (conj)

Misused

1. *The defendant claimed he was innocent, no matter his fingerprints were on the murder weapon.*
   (*Even though* should be used here.)

2. *No matter it snows, the university will not close.*
   (*If* or *whether* should follow *matter*. *Even if* instead of *no matter* would be even better.)

Correct

1. *Many voters will not support a candidate from the other party* **no matter who** *is put forward.*
   (*No matter* + question word)

2. **No matter** *the season, Vermont is a beautiful place.*
   (*No matter* the + noun)

3. *Whether she passes or fails, this will be her last semester.*
   (*No matter* isn't necessary before *whether*.)

In a nutshell: *No matter* can be followed by a *wh-* clause or a simple noun (phrase), but not a *that* clause or an independent clause.

Try writing your own sentences, one with a *wh-* clause after *no matter*, and one with a noun (phrase).

I'll leave no matter what Miao said.

Obese (adj) / Obesity (n)

Misused

1. *Obese is one of the most serious health issues among teens in the U.S.*
   (*Obese* is an adjective, not a noun, so it cannot be the subject. *Obesity* should be used here.)

2. *Many university students gain weight during their freshman year and become obesity.*
   (Here, the adjective *obese* is necessary.)

3. *The rat obesed when it was fed a high fat diet.*
   (*Obese* is not a verb. *Became obese* works here.)

Correct

1. *In spite of efforts to educate the American public about the dangers of being overweight, the percentage of Americans who are **obese** continues to rise.*

2. ***Obesity** is not just an American issue; it is becoming significant in Asia as well.*

In a nutshell: *Obese* is an adjective, and *obesity* is a noun.

Try writing your own sentences, one with the noun *obesity* and one with the adjective *obese*.

Soft drinks have been identified as a possible cause of obesity.

Being obese is dangerous for our health.

38

Occur (v$_i$)

Misused

1. *An earthquake occured in Indonesia yesterday.*
   (*Occured* is not the correct spelling. The *r* must be doubled for *occurred* or *occurring*.)

2. *A terrible tsunami was occurred in Japan in 2011.*
   (*Occur* is intransitive. It cannot be made passive.)

3. *The president occurred many tragic events during his term of office.*
   (*Occur* cannot be transitive and take a direct object.)

Correct

1. *It is nearly impossible to predict when disasters may **occur**.*

2. *Headaches often **occur** in conjunction with dehydration.*

3. *A major earthquake **occurred** in San Francisco in 1906.*

4. *A major riot is **occurring** in the prison right now.*

In a nutshell: The final *r* must be doubled for the past or continuous tense. *Occur* can never be made passive, but a *be* verb can precede it to form a continuous tense.

Try writing your own sentences, one in the past tense and one in the present continuous.

The mistake of print occurs on every page.

A new outbreak of smallpox occurred in 1661 in China.

One of the (adj. phrase)

Misused

1. *Urbanization is one of the changes in modern society.*
   (*One of the* means "a," so it should read *a change* or *one change*, unless the context somehow requires specificity, such as *one of the many changes*.)

Correct

1. *Urbanization is **one of the** most significant changes in modern society.*
   (*Most* or any other superlative will follow *one of the*.)

2. ***One of the** changes referred to in the above table is technological development.*
   (Here, *changes* is specified by the context, so *one of the* is called for.)

3. *Nutrition is **a** subject that many doctors should have studied in college but actually did not.*
   (Here, *a* is properly used instead of *one of the*.)

In a nutshell: *One of the* means "a or an," and it is less efficient. *One of the* may be used before a superlative or in a contextually specific situation.

Try writing your own sentences, one using a superlative, and one with no specificity.

Leukaemia /lju'ki:mia/ is one of the ∧cancer that cannot be cured.
    most serious

One of the ∧apples is rotten.
    biggest

40

Oppose (v$_t$) (see **Against**)

Misused

1. *The Republican Party is opposed with the tax hike.*
   (Wrong preposition. *Be opposed to* is idiomatic.)

2. *Many parents opposed to the new school uniform policy.*
   (*Oppose* is a transitive verb. When used as a verb, it needs no preposition after it.)

3. *Students protested to show their oppose to the tuition increase.*
   (*Oppose* is not a noun. *Opposition* is.)

4. *Most voters oppose the government to raise taxes.*
   (This sentence could sound like *In order to raise taxes, the citizens oppose the government.* Thus, instead of the infinitive *to raise*, the gerund *raising* should be used.)

Correct

1. *Students who **opposed** the tuition hike united to display their **opposition** in a protest at the student union.*

2. *The Catholic Church is traditionally **opposed** to birth control and abortion.*

3. *Parents generally **oppose** children's talking with strangers.*
   (Notice the gerund after *children's.*)

In a nutshell: *Oppose* is a transitive verb and requires no preposition after it. *Be opposed to* means *oppose*. When an agent is the object of *oppose*, what the agent does will be expressed in gerund form.

Try writing your own sentences, one with *oppose* and one with *be opposed to*.

The students were strongly opposed to discrimination.

A lot of people are going to be opposed to the opinion which we're going to be looking at it very strongly.

Pay attention to (phrasal v)

Misused

1. *It is important for English language learners to pay attention at grammar when they read.*
   (*Pay attention to* is idiomatic.)

2. *When taking a test, it is essential to pay attention on instructions.*
   (*Pay attention to* is idiomatic.)

3. *The students were not paying enough attention to class, so they failed to hear the professor announce the upcoming quiz.*
   (Here, **in class**, the students were *not paying attention to* the professor. *In* should follow attention. *Pay attention in* (*to* something) is situational, not idiomatic.)

Correct

1. *Students who **pay attention to** sleeping enough and eating properly often attain higher grades than those who do not.*

2. ***Paying attention to** cell phones when driving is extremely hazardous.*

3. *It is important to **pay attention** at home and at school **to** cleanliness, especially during flu season.*
   (Can you tell which prepositions are situational, and which is idiomatic?)

4. *Parents should teach their children to **pay attention** when teachers are speaking.*
   (Here, no preposition is needed at all.)

In a nutshell: *Pay attention to* is idiomatic. *To* will precede the noun that requires attention. Other prepositions may follow *pay attention* only to show the situation in which attention is being paid.

Try writing your own sentences, one with *to* and one with some other preposition and *to*.

In this materialistic age we need to pay attention to our surroundings.

⚹ pay attention in class (to) the teacher

42

changes

Percent (n) / Percentage (n)

Misused

1. *Nearly 75 percentage of adolescents spend more time texting now than speaking on the phone.*
   (*Percent* should be used after a number.)

2. *If the percent of smokers falls, national health care costs could drop dramatically.*
   (Here, *percentage* is necessary.)

Correct

1. *Heart disease accounts for more than 25* **percent** *of all deaths in the U.S.*

2. *The* **percentage** *of women who experience heart attacks is rising.*
   (Notice that *percentage* is singular.)

In a nutshell: *Percent* or % is always preceded by a number. *Percentage* means portion or fraction. No number will precede it.

Try writing your own sentences, one with *percent* and one with *percentage*.

This compone gives a 10 percent discount.

~~Text~~ Internet attracts a large percentage of the teenages.

Present (v$_t$/adj)

Misused

1. *Table 1 presents that the market share of Company X has increased.*
   (*Present* can't take a *that* clause as its object.)

2. *The lecturer presented that new antibiotic-resistant bacteria have developed.*
   (*Present* can't take a *that* clause as its object.)

3. *Thirty students presented in class, and only two were absent.*
   (The adjective *present*, meaning "not absent," cannot be made into a verb.
   A *be* verb is required.)

Correct

1. *Table 1 **presents** data that clearly shows that the market share of Company X has increased.*

2. *The lecturer **presented** information about new strains of antibiotic-resistant bacteria.*

3. *Thirty students **were present** in the class.*

In a nutshell: The verb *present* cannot precede a *that* clause. The adjective *present* requires a *be* verb before it.

Try writing your own sentences, one with the verb and one with the adjective.

Oxygen is present in the bloodstream.

Smoking is not relevant to the present problem.

Proud (adj) / Pride (n/v$_t$)

Misused

1. *China prouds its rapid modernization in the 21st century.*
   (*Proud* is not a verb, but it is an adjective. *Is proud of* works here.)

2. *The executive was proud the accomplishments of the company.*
   (*Of* should follow *was* (be) *proud* when a noun follows it.)

3. *The university was pride of its faculty.*
   (The adjective *proud*, not the noun *pride*, is necessary here.)

4. *Most parents take pride of their children.*
   (Wrong preposition. *Take pride in* is idiomatic.)

Correct

1. *New York City **is proud of** its championship football team.*

2. *Teachers take **pride** in their students' accomplishments.*

3. *Cats seem to **pride** themselves in their cleanliness.*
   (Not so common but nevertheless correct usage of *pride* as a
   verb + reflexive pronoun + *in*.)

In a nutshell: *Proud* is an adjective, and not a verb. If there is a noun after it, the preposition *of* will be used. *Pride* is a noun that occurs often in the idiomatic expression *take pride in*.

Try writing your own sentences, one with the adjective *proud* and one with the noun *pride*.

Ellan is proud of her family ~~for their support~~. Which from the royal courts of Europe.

The pride of the village is the University.

45   Reason (n)

Misused

1. *The reason why oil prices have increased is* ~~because~~ *that a pipeline broke.*
   (Some native speakers may speak like this, but it is somewhat illogical.
   The broken pipeline is the reason, not the cause of the reason.)

2. *Oil prices skyrocketed* ~~because of~~ *for three reasons.*
   (*For three reasons* is much more idiomatic and less awkward.)   The reason for

   ✱

3. *Three reasons exist why the earth will probably cool in the future.*
   (This sentence can be understood, but it is awkward.)

4. *Global warming is caused by several reasons.*
   (Factors would be better. Reasons are mental activity.)

Correct

1. *Oil prices have increased because a major pipeline broke.*
   (*Reason* is not needed at all. This sentence is more efficient than #2 below.)

2. *The **reason** why oil prices have risen is that a major pipeline broke.*
   (While grammatical and logical, this sentence is a bit inefficient.)

3. *Oil prices skyrocketed for three **reason**s.*

4. *The earth will probably cool in the future for three **reasons**.*

5. *The **reason** for the stock market crash was careless speculation.*
   (This sentence sounds more efficient and academic than #5 above.)

In a nutshell: *For* ___ *reasons* is used rather than *because of* ___ *reasons.*

Try writing your own sentences using *reason for* and *reason why* or a reduced *why* clause.

There was no obvious reason for the traffic accident.

_____

_____

_____

Relax (v$_i$/v$_t$) / Relaxed (adj) / Relaxing (adj)
(cause) (feeler)

Misused

1. *To relieve symptoms of stress, it is important to relax oneself.*
   (*Relax* can be an intransitive verb. No object is necessary here.)

2. *Trade regulations should be relax.*
   (*Relax* can be transitive. Here it should be the passive form,
   be relaxed.)

3. *Sitting in a hot tub is relaxed.*
   ("Sitting" doesn't feel anything. The person doing the sitting feels *relaxed*.
   Whatever causes the *relaxed* feeling is *relaxing*.)

4. *While some feel stressed when driving, others feel relaxing.*
   (Here, the person doing the feeling is the subject, so *relaxed* is needed.)

Correct

1. *Taking a hot bath enables muscles to **relax**.*

2. *With a decreased threat of terrorism, airport security measures can be **relaxed**.*

3. *It is **relaxing** to drink warm milk before sleeping.*

4. *Instead of looking nervous in the interview, the applicant appeared **relaxed**.*

5. *Drivers should **relax** the grip on the steering wheel to prevent over-steering.*
   (Here, *relax* is used transitively.)

In a nutshell: *Relax* can be intransitive, so reflexive pronouns are unnecessary. *Relaxing* describes something outside the feeler, and *relaxed* describes the feeler.

Try writing your own sentences, one with *relax*, one with *relaxing*, and one with *relaxed*.

My idea of paradise is to relax on the seafront.

The crowds relaxed into laughter at the speaker's # excellent joke

He plans to have a relaxing vacation.

47 Research (n)

Misused

1. *Several researches have been carried out to investigate the effects of classical music on the intelligence of children.*
   (*Research* is not countable, so it cannot be made plural. *Investigation* and *study* are countable synonyms of *research* and can be used here in the plural.)

2. *A research conducted at the University of Delaware confirmed the hypothesis.*
   (*Research* is not countable, so *a* cannot modify it.)

3. *It is necessary to do more research on the long-term effects of this medicine.*
   (While not ungrammatical, *do* is a relatively unsophisticated verb. *Conduct* or even *carry out* would be better.)

Correct

1. *A variety of **research** has investigated the effects of classical music on the intelligence of children.*

2. ***Research** conducted by Smith produced intriguing results.*

3. *More **research** on the long-term effects is necessary.*

In a nutshell: *Research* is not countable, so *a* or *several* cannot be used with it, and it cannot be made plural. *Conduct* is an appropriate academic verb to use with *research*.

Try writing your own sentences with *research*, using *conduct* in one of them.

Global Warming is the core of our research.

Safe (adj) / safety (n)

Misused

1. *Compared to smaller vehicles, larger ones provide greater safe.*
   (*Safe* is an adjective. The noun *safety* is needed here.)

2. *Large vehicles provide a smooth and safety ride.*
   (*Smooth* is an adjective, so parallel structure and the fact that *ride* is a noun demand the adjective *safe* be used, rather than the noun *safety*.)

Correct

1. *Larger vehicles provide greater **safety** than smaller ones.*

2. *Larger vehicles are usually considered **safer than** smaller ones.*
   (The adjective *safe* can be changed into its comparative form *safer*.)

3. *Large vehicles provide a smooth and **safe** ride.*

In a nutshell: *Safe* is an adjective, and *safety* is a noun.

Try writing your own sentences, one with the adjective and one with the noun.

This strategy is safe and satisfactory for the businessmen to achieve their targets.

It is significant to put on the ~~seatbe~~ safety belts

49

Same (n) / **Similar** (adj)

Misused

1. *Watching movies is not as same as reading the stories in books.*
   (The idiomatic expression is ***the*** *same as*.)

2. *Chemistry majors do not take the same introductory chemistry course with non-majors.*
   (The idiomatic expression is *the same **as***, not *with*.)

3. *The police officer and the lawyer were talking to a same man.*
   (*The* always comes before *same*.)

4. *The similar item made by a different company is considerably less expensive.*
   (*A*, not *the*, should come before *similar*. There may be many items similar to another, but they may differ in many ways, so *a* is used with similar.)

5. *Running shoes are similar with walking shoes, but they are slightly different.*
   (The idiomatic expression is *be similar **to***, not *with*.)

Correct

1. *The vitamin C in tablets is usually **the same** molecule **as** the vitamin C in food.*

2. *The **same** key opens the door and the trunk of the car.*

3. *A **similar** dress was on display at the department store, and it was on sale.*

4. *Cats are surprisingly **similar to** dogs.*

In a nutshell: *The* precedes *same*, and *a* precedes *similar*.

Try writing your own sentences, one with *same* and one with *similar*.

We do the same work day after day.

Miao is similar to me because we have the same aim.

Search (v$_t$/n)

Misused

1. *To write a research paper, it is necessary to search sources on the Internet and in the library.*
   (*Search* requires *for* when it means "to look for.")

Correct

1. *Police **searched** the crime scene **for** clues that might lead to the perpetrator.*
   (Notice that the police are not looking for the crime scene; they are looking in the crime scene *searching **for*** clues. The structure is "*search* place *for* thing.")

2. *The group **searched** the Internet for hours, but could not find the image they **were searching for**.*
   (Some grammarians might not like ending a sentence with a preposition, in which case they would advise *the image **for which** they **were searching**.*)

3. *The **search** for survivors of the earthquake lasted two weeks.*

In a nutshell: *Search* is used with *for* to mean "looking for something." *Search* can be used with no preposition to mean "look carefully in something." It can also be a noun.

Try writing your own sentences, one with the noun, one meaning "look for," and one meaning "look in."

- The birds were searching for a warmer climes.
- Their search for the plane is fruitless.

Stress (n/v_t) / Stressed (adj) / Stressful (adj)

Misused

1. *University life causes many stresses for students.*
   (*Stress* is naturally not countable. *Much stress* will work. *Considerable stress* or *tremendous amounts of stress* would sound even more academic.)

2. *Many bank employees have been stressful since the economic crisis of 2008.*
   (The employees feel the *stress*, so they are *stressed*.)

3. *Organic Chemistry 301 is an extremely stressed course.*
   (The course feels no stress; the students do. The course is *stressful*.)

4. *The physical education teacher stressed on fitness and skill.*
   (*Stress* is a transitive verb, and doesn't take a preposition.)

Correct

1. *There is little evidence that life is less **stressful** than it was 50 years ago.*

2. *Increased **stress** can lead to physical ailments and disease.*

3. *Physical exercise is strongly recommended for those who are **stressed**.*

4. *This course **stresses** both grammar and vocabulary.*

In a nutshell: *Stress* is generally not countable. It can be a transitive verb that means "to emphasize." *Stressful* describes something outside the feeler, while *stressed* describes the feeler.

Try writing your own sentences, one using the noun, one using the verb, and one using each form of the adjective of *stress*.

- The roof couldn't(not) bear the stress of the snow.
- The book encourage the police men through those stressful days.
- The new teacher feels stressed to have a meeting with 40 students.

Success (n) / Succeed (v$_i$)

Misused

1. *There is much pressure on students to success in college.*
   (The verb *succeed* is needed, not the noun *success*.)

2. *Succeed is the goal of every entrepreneur.*
   (The noun *success* is needed as the subject of the sentence.)

3. *High grades in college do not guarantee success on a future career.*
   (The preposition before *career* should be *in*.)

4. *The student did not succeed in her final exam.*
   (Here, the preposition should be *on*.)

Correct

1. *Innumerable factors would have to work together for the campaign **to succeed**.*

2. *Innovation is often an important factor in the formula for **success**.*

3. ***Success** on this test will mean **success** in this course, but it will not guarantee **success** in my field or in my future career.*

In a nutshell: *Success* is a noun, and *succeed* is a verb. The preposition after *succeed* depends on the noun after it.

Try writing your own sentences, one using the noun *success* and another using the verb *succeed*.

- There is an inseparable relationship between opportunity and success.
- The emperor has no son to succeed to the throne.

The key to (phrasal prep)

Misused

1. *Time management is the key to succeed in college.*
   (The *to* after *key* is a preposition, so it requires an object; that is, a noun, not a verb. The noun *success* would be correct here.)

2. *Beginning early is the key to finish assignments on time.*
   (Here, the verb *finish* must be changed to its gerund form *finishing* to become the object of the preposition.)

Correct

1. *Two generations ago, it was said that cooking was **the key to** a man's heart, but that saying might not be true today.*

2. ***The key to** fishing is patience.*

3. *Reading skill is **the key to** academic success.*

In a nutshell: *The key to* ends with the preposition *to*, so it will be followed by a noun. If an action is desired, it must be expressed in the gerund form.

Try writing your own sentences, one with a simple noun after *the key to* and one with a gerund.

· Miao lost the key to the dormitory for twice.

· Communication is the key to a relationship.

54

Through (prep) / Throughout (prep)

Misused

1. *The Internet allows information to quickly travel through the world.*
   (The information flows in all directions, so *throughout* is more appropriate.)

2. *Many lessons can be learned through life.*
   (The most probable meaning here is "at every point of life," no matter where one goes or what one does; thus, *throughout* is more appropriate.)

3. *The protagonist grew throughout that experience.*
   (Here, the experience is best understood as a point or unit in time, rather than a series of points; thus, *through* is more appropriate.)

Correct

1. ***Through** the Internet, a story can spread throughout the world almost instantaneously.*
   (*Through* is used with a vehicle or medium.)

2. ***Through** a stroke of luck, the inventor hit on the proper material for his machine.*

3. *Many keen insights appeared **throughout** the research paper.*

In a nutshell: *Through* implies a single direction, perhaps in a medium or by a vehicle. *Throughout* implies all directions and everywhere.

Try writing your own sentences, one with *through* and one with *throughout*.

· The deaf communicate through body language.

· Miao has remained smilling throughout the interview.

Trustworthy (adj)

Misused

1. *That author seems extremely trustable.*
   (*Trustable* is not a word; *trustworthy* is.)

Correct

1. *That salesman has such a huge number of customers because he is so* **trustworthy**.

2. *"Honesty is the best policy" is a* **trustworthy** *statement.*
   (Notice that *trustworthy* can be used to describe both people and things.)

In a nutshell: *Trustable* is not a word. *Trustworthy* is an adjective.

Try writing your own sentences with *trustworthy*.

It is generally admitted that Miao is a thrustworthy person.

Use (n/v) / Usage (n)

Misused

1. *The usage of fossil fuels leads to global warming.*
   (*Using* or *the use of* would be better. *Usage* tends to be related to how something is used or how much, rather than the act of using itself.)

2. *The usage of defensive specialists has changed the game of volleyball.*
   (Here also, the sentence is referring to the fact that they are used, rather than how or how much. Thus, *use* would be better.)

Correct

1. *Electricity **usage** has tripled in the past 40 years.*

2. *To truly know a word means to know not only the meaning of a word but also its **usage**.*

3. *A jack-knife has many **uses**; thus, campers often carry them.*

In a nutshell: *Usage* tends to be related to how something is used or how much. *Use* refers more to the act of *using* something.

Try writing your own sentences, one with *usage* and one with *use*.

Shoes ~~will~~ break broke under rough usage.

I use boiled water to exterminate mice.

57 Whereas (conj)

Misused

1. *Whereas apples require cross-fertilization.*
   (This sentence is a fragment.)

2. *It is commonly believed that George Washington once confessed to cutting down a cherry tree; whereas, he did not.*
   (*Whereas* is used for contrasts, not contradictions. *However* is more appropriate here.)

3. *Whereas Republicans, who generally advocate military spending, Democrats generally favor social spending.*
   (Because of the *who* clause, the *whereas* clause becomes a fragment. *Unlike* would be better; or eliminating *, who* would also work.)

Correct

1. ***Whereas** oranges require relatively warm climates to thrive, apples can produce well in cooler conditions.*

2. *Many Asian cultures tend to be group-oriented, **whereas** American culture tends to be individualistic.*
   (Notice that the *whereas* clause can be at the beginning or at the end.)

In a nutshell: *Whereas* is used to show contrasts rather than contradictions, and it introduces dependent clauses.

Try writing your own sentences, one with *whereas* as the first word and one with it later in the sentence.

Some residents praise him, whereas others condemn him.

Whereas I want a house other students want a flat.

Whether (conj)

Misused

---

1. *It is uncertain whether that the medicine actually cured the woman; her recovery may have been due to the placebo effect.*
   (*That* is unnecessary after *whether*.)

2. *Whether will he win the election or not, his campaign has certainly impacted the outcome.*
   (The noun clause *he wins* should follow *whether*, not the question *will he win*.)

Correct

---

1. *It is difficult to determine beforehand **whether** the policy will be effective or not.*
   (*Or not* is optional.)

2. *Many casually wondered **whether** the world would actually end on December 21, 2012.*

3. *The president is considering **whether** to run for a second term of office.*
   (Notice the infinitive after *whether*.)

4. *The author enjoyed compiling his work, **whether** or not it would ever be published.*

In a nutshell: A *that* clause will not follow *whether*. *Whether* begins a noun or infinitive clause.

Try writing your own sentences, one with an infinitive and one with a noun clause after *whether*.

It is doubtful whether it is true or not

Whether on the platform or beyond it, the girl works hard.

59

While (conj) / **during** (prep)

Misused

---

1. *During he was visiting England, the tourist visited Stonehenge.*
   (*During* is a preposition and must have a noun as its object. *While* should
   be used instead of *during*.)

2. *While summer vacation, many students travel, but others continue to take courses.*
   (*While* must be followed by a clause or a reduced clause. *During* would be correct
   here.)

Correct

---

1. ***During*** *the test, cell phone use is not permitted.*

2. ***While*** *walking to work yesterday, the secretary broke the heel of her shoe.*
   (This sentence contains a reduced clause. Can you identify it?)

3. ***While*** *the students were taking the test, the professor was monitoring all that was
   happening in the room.*

4. ***While*** *many believe video games are harmless, some researchers are finding evidence
   that they really can be quite dangerous.*
   (*While* can be used to introduce a contrast.)

In a nutshell: A noun or noun phrase will follow *during*. A clause will follow *while*. *While* can
also be used to contrast.

Try writing your own sentences, one using a comparison, one using a clause or reduced clause, and
one using a noun or noun phrase after *while* or *during*.

· That was a great while ago, the queen had a baby that was called snow white.

· They do not smoke while driving.

· During summer, the students will give five performances

Worthy (adj) / worthwhile (adj)

Misused

1. *It is worthy to study engineering because engineers earn high salaries.*
   (Here, *worthwhile* should be used to mean "it is an effective use of time and effort.")

2. *The president is worthy to vote for.*
   (*Be worth ____ -ing* is idiomatic.)

3. *It is worthwhile jogging every day.*
   (An infinitive after *worthwhile* is a better choice.)

4. *A leader who puts his followers ahead of himself is worthwhile to praise.*
   (*Worthwhile* is used with activities that require time and effort. The verb is *is*, so an adjective must refer to the leader. *Worthy of praise* would work.)

Correct

1. *It **is worthwhile to** study English because it can be used worldwide.*

2. *This computer **is worth** buying even if it is somewhat expensive.*

3. *It **is worthwhile to** review vocabulary often.*

4. *A political leader who willingly steps down from power **is worthy of** praise.*

5. *It may be **worth your while** to read through this book periodically to improve your academic writing.*
   (Notice how *worth* and *while* are separated here by *your*. It is a somewhat unusual usage, but it is grammatical, and it is offered here as a bonus.)

In a nutshell: *Worth* can be followed by a gerund, *worthwhile* describes an activity that is a profitable use of time or effort, and *worthy* means deserving.

Try writing your own sentences, one using ⟨worthy⟩, one using ⟨worthwhile⟩, and one using ⟨worth⟩

· This teacher is worthy to be revered.

· It is worthwhile to do the expensive trade.

· The worth of higher education is ~~opening a better life~~ occupation. facilitating the development of ~~society~~ social morality.

ELT Books and Study Guides

Wayzgoose Press publishes a popular line of self-study ebooks and audiobooks for students of English as a second language as well as specialized textbooks and workbooks for English teachers. Find the full range of current titles, including guides for practicing reading, writing, grammar, speaking, listening, grammar, and vocabulary, on our website.

To be notified about new titles and special contests, events, and sales from Wayzgoose Press, please visit our website at http://wayzgoosepress.com and sign up for our mailing list. (We send email infrequently, and you can unsubscribe at any time.)

Made in the USA
Middletown, DE
05 March 2019